From Beaten Employee to Proud Owner

Gain the will to start a business, control your destiny, and never apply for another job again

Cory Galbraith

DEDICATION

This book is dedicated to every hard-working person who has ever been unjustly fired or laid off from their employment and who now faces the opportunity to start a new life of self-sufficiency.

CONTENTS

ACKNOWLEDGMENT

This book is the result of 30 years in the trenches. But I need to acknowledge one special person, my wife, whose support has made my journey in business possible.

1 INTRODUCTION

On a warm summer day in 1993, I went to work with a smile on my face, ready to tackle the day. I loved my job as a journalist and editor. It wasn't what I wanted to do for the rest of my life, but for that period of time, it was perfect. I had a baby on the way. My wife and I had recently purchased our new home.

As I reviewed my to-do list that morning and sipped on my coffee, there was a knock at the door. It was the company general manager. But he wasn't alone. The other man introduced himself as the company lawyer. I had an uncomfortable feeling. And then it happened. I was fired.

After three years of loyal service, I was humiliated by being escorted out of the building, thrown out like garbage.

It was a scene that gets played out every day in offices around the globe.

Today – millennials new to the workforce, disenchanted with the archaic hierarchy of an uncaring corporate entity, and older workers displaced because of age discrimination, feeling tossed aside despite a lifetime of corporate knowledge and experience – face the same opportunity – to go it alone.

But how exactly?

When I decided to embark on a journey of business ownership, none of the books at the time could answer that question in any meaningful way. There was a lack of real-world practical advice. The books were long on explaining my dilemma, short on solutions.

They were void of humor. They didn't challenge me. Most were written by academics. Not people who had actually learned from running a business. And of the few real business owners who did write books, there was a disconnect. They seemed to be talking to people who already had a mature business, or who at least had some experience. But I was at point zero. They also seemed more interested in promoting their own celebrity than helping me.

Not much has changed since those days. In fact, there is now more hype, more bad information and more ill-conceived advice than ever.

This book is an attempt to counter all of that, and offer what I hope will be a catalyst for you to act in your own best interest – to become self-sufficient through the low-risk approach I recommend.

This is not a book on how to become a millionaire or launch the biggest and best company in the world. It is far less ambitious and glamorous. Instead, it's about how you can make a good living on your own.

Throughout these pages, I refer to "business ownership" "self-employment" and "independent contracting". Essentially, within the context of the book, they are the same. The objective is to discard the tired, old and largely inefficient approach to acquiring an income – that of doing it via a "job" – and replace it with starting and running a successful service business.

Why a "service" business? Because for most people reading this book, launching a product or manufacturing business is both out of reach and, in my view, too risky.

The formula I propose in this book is not for people who are willing to risk everything they have for an unproven idea. Rather, it's a guide on how to offer known services that people need. I believe it to be a much more sound, practical route to take, compared to the wild pursuits we hear about in the media.

Everything in this book has been tested by me over three decades of trial and error. This is not a book about theory. It's about the real world.

If I've done my job, after reading this book, you will at least consider self-employment as a viable option. May it be a journey filled with reward – both financially and personally.

Let's get started.

2 IT'S ONLY A MATTER OF TIME BEFORE YOU'RE PUSHED OUT

As you read this - somebody, somewhere - is getting fired for an unjust cause. It may be because the boss simply didn't like the way you looked at her or him. It might be because you dared to question the boss's authority.

Firings, seemingly at the whim of the manager, are taking place at an alarming rate. And in many jurisdictions, it's entirely legal. "Employment at will" is now standard in a number of states allowing termination for any reason, or more often than not - no reason at all. (Usually, "no reason" is given as the cause to avoid legal action).

In Canada, where "employment at will" does not exist, some provincial employment standards still allow firing for no reason under certain circumstances, a fact that surprises most Canadians. In the UK, you can generally only challenge a dismissal if you've been employed full time for at least two years. And according to the International Trade Union Confederation, 84 countries have no labor laws at all for specified groups of employees - allowing not only unjust dismissal, but violence against workers as well.

The U.S. Bureau of Labor Statistics reports that the average employee tenure is now only three to four years.

Sooner or later, one way or the other, you're going to be let go.

And if it's not a firing, then it'll be a layoff.

Back in 1979, less than five per cent of Fortune 100 companies resorted to layoffs to save money. But according to a McMaster University study, that figure shot up to 45 per cent by 1994. Another survey of 2,000 large firms, by McKinsey, found that a whopping 65 per cent of those firms had implemented large-scale lay-offs from 2008 to 2011.

Today, if you read the headlines, you'll likely find at least one story of a massive layoff. And how do people typically react when they're laid off? Shock, sadness, extreme anxiety and panic. If they were "realists" they would expect to be laid off, knowing it's just a matter of time.

Allow me to make this bold statement right now:

Working for somebody else is riskier than working for yourself.

Consider this. As an employee, you have a single source of income. As a business owner, you have multiple sources of income. If you have ten clients, that's like having ten employers or potentially, ten times your income. In the event your employer cuts you off, you're left with nothing. But, as a business owner, if one of the ten clients stops using you, you still have nine others.

Even if your business made little money, and was struggling - you would still be in a better scenario than if you put your livelihood, and the security of your family, in the hands of a corporate entity that didn't care about you - and doesn't even know your name.

You're just a number.

But what if you were a president, CEO or other top-level executive? Surely, you would have greater job security then. No, you would not. In fact, you may have less security because a lot is riding at the top of the heap. You're still just an employee, reporting either to the Chairperson, or a Board of Directors, so there's still the opportunity to get sacked, and often it can be just because you looked at somebody the wrong way. Or a new member of the board may simply not like you.

In one of the most famous firings of all time, Ford Motor Company President Lee Iacocca was fired by the then Chairman, Henry Ford II because Ford said, "Sometimes, you just don't like somebody."

Another bold statement:

As a small business owner, you are more secure than the CEO of the largest companies.

Putting the statistics aside, in all of us is the deeply embedded desire and need to feed ourselves and our families. It's a basic requirement, and as human beings, one could argue - a right. We should not have to live, on a daily basis, with the threat, that at any moment, our very survival will be put into jeopardy.

There is also the need for control. When we put the survival and dignity of ourselves and our families into the hands of a corporate boardroom, we are giving up 100 per cent control.

One could argue that if you do a great job in the workplace, the chances of being let go are reduced. That may have been the case long ago. It's not the case now. Some of the hardest working and most talented people are tossed aside. When it comes to corporate reorganization, often those making the most money have a target on their back.

It's time we did away with delusional thinking - that somehow, because we're "good," we are protected.

Total control can only come through self-employment.

But it's not just about security and control. It's also having the opportunity to do work that gives you a purpose. You can spend years doing work that gives you no meaning. Or, you can take a chance on yourself, and do the kind of work you've always wanted to do - helping other people and making this a better planet in which to live.

If you've been fired or laid off, they did you a favor

The day after I had been fired, I vowed that never again would anyone have that kind of power over me. I was determined to take matters into my own hands and control my own destiny. (In my case, the firing was because I had the nerve to tell my co-workers that I wanted to one day run my own business. How dare I say such a thing!)

If you've been recently fired or laid off, you must view this is a good thing - a message that your time has come to become self-sufficient.

And make no mistake. You must become self-sufficient. You can no longer put your blind faith in a system that is designed to reject you, over and over again, no matter your talents, skills, enthusiasm and intelligence.

I was one of the many people who only entered into self-employment after being terminated from a job. My motivation was anger and that can be a good thing if it causes you to take action.

Don't be sad. Get mad. Then act.

3 GET OUT OF THAT CRAZY PLACE

If you don't get fired or laid off, it's likely you'll want to leave anyway.

Bad bosses who were promoted because of their technical expertise but never trained on how to manage teams; insane policies, such as having to sign in to grab a paperclip, sending the message that you can't be trusted; a lack of direction and feedback; never-ending meetings with no outcomes; and a general lack of respect and validation - all lead people to hate where they work.

The stats are shocking. The Gallup organization reported that in 2017, 85 per cent of the world's workers hated their jobs (a little better than four years earlier when it was 90 per cent). The figure in the U.S. was a bit less, although still unacceptably high at 70 per cent.

The Gallup poll made the point that it wasn't so much the company that people despised. It was their boss.

Another survey by Robert Half in the UK found that people begin to hate their jobs around age 35. One of the main findings was that people feel unappreciated.

Participants of the surveys also said they couldn't concentrate at work due to noise and interruptions. Many were woefully unhappy, experienced a lack of friends and support in the workplace, and were stressed beyond the breaking point.

The corporate office, it would seem, is not meant for human beings. It's an insane place.

You'll have many of your own horror stories of workplace insanity. But here are two quick examples from my days in the trenches that showcase just how corporations see you as an employee, and how they would likely view you if you became a business owner.

Your ideas will be heard

As an employee, my ideas were never heard.

I was, after all, just a lowly pion - one of many expected to do what I was told. Certainly not make any suggestions.

I would eventually leave the company, and fortunately, it was on good terms. So good in fact, that a mere six months later, I was hired by the firm to be an outside consultant for a few weeks.

Then something unbelievable happened.

I forwarded the exact same ideas that I had a year earlier to the same executives - but this time, everyone thought my ideas were, in the words of one manager, "fantastic!".

As a general rule, large corporations have much more respect for outside consultants and independent contractors than they do their own people.

You'll be a bum one day, working from within - and a genius the next, working from the outside.

Turf protection

In my second example - I was walking down the hallway of the large corporation where I had once worked, making my way from the cafeteria. Going in the other direction, on his way to the cafeteria, was, of all people, the president. We bumped into each other. The perfect opportunity I felt, to relay a few of my ideas. The president listened intently and said, "We'll need to follow up."

I was elated. Recognition from the top! This was a big positive for our department so I informed my immediate supervisor. But much to my surprise, she wasn't happy. Not happy at all. I was told, "You never speak to the president directly! Only I can speak to the president!"

My happiness turned to embarrassment, guilt and confusion. Then I thought about how ludicrous this was. She was actually telling me that I could not speak to another human being. An innocent exchange in a hallway. That's all it was.

I asked myself - is this the kind of place I want to work?

A short time later, as a business consultant, I was free to talk with whomever I chose.

There are chains on you as an employee.

Get the respect you deserve

If you can't get respect on the inside, be on the outside.

Former employers will view you much differently because they're not stupid. They know that if you're surviving on your own, without the protection (or more accurately, the "abuse") of the "mother corporation" then you have to be doing something right.

Even the top executives of the corporation have not done what you've done - striking it out on your own. Yes, they may be making a lot more money than you. They may have a big pension. They may have status.

But you have something they do not - freedom from the threat of termination.

4 DEBUNKING EXCUSES AND MYTHS

Whether you've been tossed out, or left voluntarily - how can you adjust your mindset to enter the world of working for yourself? It's not an easy transition. It can be scary. So, what most people do is make up excuses in order to justify their return to the traditional workforce.

The excuses and the myths that prevent people from starting a business are limitless. In this chapter, I will highlight some of the most common mental barriers, and take apart each one of them, so you can acquire the necessary mindset – one of confidence - to make an informed decision on whether or not to pursue independence, or the alternative – a life of corporate torture.

Firstly - there is an enormous myth floating around out there, perpetuated by so-called business gurus, many of whom have never actually run a business, and by existing insecure business owners with poor ethics who would rather you not start a business because you'll then be competing with them.

The myth is this: *starting and running a business is not for everyone.*

What they really should be saying is:

Running a business is not for everyone who is lazy, ignorant, incompetent or lacking confidence.

That would be a far more accurate statement.

Because if you are willing to work hard, if you have a burning desire to learn, to be disciplined and to put faith in yourself - then yes, ANYONE can start and run a successful business.

We cannot use the excuse that some people are not cut out for this, and maybe we are among them so we'll give up our God given right to protect ourselves and our families, and just leave fate in the hands of the ambassadors of greed who will toss us away without even an ounce of guilt.

A number of years ago, a director in a large corporation asked me out to lunch and revealed that he'd had enough of corporate politics and wanted advice on how to start a business. As is often the case, there was a "but". This is typically followed by a long stream of excuses. "But I am too busy." Really? He was too busy to become self-sufficient? "But I don't know what I'm doing." Nobody does in the beginning. Knowledge is the key to carving a pathway (and that's what this book is all about).

The biggest excuse of all is: "I don't think I can do it." Essentially, when people say this, it's code for "I don't believe in myself." I have talked to CEOs and high-level managers, making six figures, who say they can't do it. People who have accomplished a great deal working for others, shrink into an infantile position in which they purport to now be a grade A idiot with no skill set, no ideas and no capabilities.

Dig deep into your soul

We need to dig deep inside of ourselves to see the truth. Throughout this book, I will challenge your assumptions about yourself – those that prevent you from moving forward. I'm going to fight you, every step of the way, when you tell me that you can't do it. Because that's just not true. It's a lie.

If we are as incapable as we tell ourselves, how did we accomplish any of the things we've done so far? Not just in the workplace but life in general?

Your inner voice will torture you with the question "Who do I think I am?" You're a person who deserves life-long security. And if you don't do this for yourself, then do it for the people you love. Because the day you're fired or laid off will likely be followed by weeks, months or even years of unemployment.

When I tell people the real reason that they're not pursuing their dream of self-employment is a lack of confidence, they get very insulted. "That's not true!" We have a brain that is far more powerful than we realize. We have so little faith in it, even though it's capable of getting us out of almost any jam. That brain of yours can learn the "how" part of going out on your own. It's time we trusted the power that exists above our shoulders.

What if I'm successful?

Many people do not start a business (despite claiming that they want to) because deep down, they are afraid of - not failure, but of success.

Will I lose my friends? You might lose a few, but if you do, were they really friends in the first place? What if I become a different person? Yes, you will change, but for the better. How will I spend the money? You will reinvest it in the business and you will enjoy self-sufficiency.

The best way to deal with fear of success is to adopt a humble perspective, which is to say, "I likely won't become widely successful anyway." And guess what? You won't. Not at the beginning. If anything, you'll struggle out of the gate. And that's okay. Because it's going to take up to a full year for your business to start flying. Count on it.

We all have a different definition of success. For the purposes of this book - making a living and providing for yourself and your family through your own sweat equity - is success. If you're good with that definition, keep reading. If you're not good with it, then this book will be of no use to you and you may as well just put it down and start looking for some crummy "job" out there and wait to be terminated. (I go as far as to say that when a company hires you, they've already started to get rid of you).

But most small businesses fail

We've all heard the numbers. The U.S. Small Business Administration reports that over half of all small businesses fail in the first year, and 95 per cent - the vast majority – fail within five years.

In a social media posting I recently made asking unemployed people to consider self-employment, one person angrily wrote back that my advice was bad because he did just that and lost all of his money. He was among the 95 per cent. But he didn't learn what was necessary to keep his operation afloat. He then had the nerve to say because he couldn't make it, nobody could. The epitome of arrogance.

Please do not listen to people who try to stop you before you've even started.

Here is the important lesson. If you're struggling, you can always change direction.

The business I run today (live streaming) was never in my plans. It's not the business that I set out to run. You need to keep an open mind and listen to clients. The business I have now was the result of a client's need to reach more of their customers. They asked me: "Can you do live streaming?" Answer: "Yes". In fact, I had no idea what live streaming even was. But if this client needed it, I figured so too would many others. I did the research. Hired the right people. And now, after 15 years, I am most certainly not part of the 95 per cent who disappeared.

The people who tell you they've tried it - and it doesn't work - are negative, bitter, resentful and quite likely, hoping you'll fail too, so they can validate their position.

You will be told that the economy is bad; that there isn't any security in running a business; and that you'll go broke. Listen to none of it.

This book is about how to avoid being in the small business failure statistics. There are many good reasons why all those businesses are disappearing. But the primary reason is that they failed to fine-tune – to change direction when required.

Running your own show is not about taking risks. To the contrary, it's about eliminating risk, and when opportunities present themselves, taking calculated risks.

You don't need money

One of the great fallacies is that you need a lot of money to start a business. Nothing could be farther from the truth.

Let's acknowledge that anyone can start a business. They can acquire a business license and open up a business bank account, produce business cards and call themselves an owner or CEO (Chief Executive Officer). The vast majority of "CEOs" on LinkedIn and other social media platforms are, in fact, people who are running a one-person or maybe two-person operation, hiding in a basement some place, more or less "pretending". Worse yet, there are many so-called "Presidents" in charge of nothing - with a business in name only, not an actual going concern.

Very few of these people spent any money on setting up their "business." And it is entirely possible to create a real business, with real clients and real projects, also with very little money. In fact, I strongly recommend that you don't spend any money.

You may have seen entrepreneurs on Shark Tank and other similar business investment shows in which the people making the pitch reveal that they've spent all of their money, or have borrowed insane amounts of money, and yet do not have a single sale - or even any hope of getting a sale.

Do not. I repeat - do not spend more than a few hundred dollars in setting up your business.

Do not mortgage your house. Do not borrow large sums of money. Don't spend all of your money buying a franchise. Don't buy an existing business. Do not ask your parents for money (yes - I know that Jeff Bezos did that to start Amazon) and do not spend your savings buying fancy furniture, trying to create the facade of success.

There are "gurus" who will tell you that you must spend money to make money. It is the stuff of nonsense and it saddens me that so many people buy into this, only to lose everything.

For the vast majority of people, starting a "service" business, in which they are the labor (certainly for the start-up phase), is by far, the best way to go. You won't be spending any money on employees and fancy offices. You'll be doing everything yourself, keeping your expenses to a rock bottom level.

As I write this, a friend of mine is starting a business that requires a considerable amount of equipment. I have urged her not to purchase any of it in this critical start-up phase. Instead, rent what is needed per job and build the rental costs into the quote.

You need to keep as much money in your pocket as possible in order to allow your little operation to breathe. Otherwise, you're going to choke it. You will choke it to death, because cash is like blood to a business. And I want you to have that blood flowing through your corporate veins.

In the process of doing all of the many tasks for a start-up business, keeping costs low, you will learn a great deal. In addition to being self-sufficient, you'll undergo profound personal growth, becoming a smarter, more rounded version of yourself.

And that's worth all of the money in the world.

There is no perfect time to start a business (and no bad time)

Planning to start a business? I have a friend who has been planning to start a business for 20 years. But it's never going to happen. I know that. He knows it too, deep down.

That's because procrastinating is really a form of insecurity. Putting this major decision off indefinitely is an admission that we lack confidence. It's fear of the unknown.

When I asked my friend why he has been waiting for so long to get started, he responded: "I'm waiting for the right time. Now is not good."

The perfect moment will, of course, never arrive.

The "right" time is always now.

I can't compete with big business

Actually, this subheading should read "Big business can't compete with you."

Corporations are large, bloated slow moving creatures. Contrary to what most of us believe, a good number of them are not even technically advanced. (How many offices are still using Internet Explorer 11?).

The big guys don't care much about customer service. In fact, as a customer, you're a problem. Multi-national firms show us advertising that we love to hate, and that we just don't believe. Corporations are painfully slow at getting back to us. They hide behind web sites.

Many are not socially responsible, despite demands from the buying public.

And to top it all off, they're not very friendly.

Never before has there been so much opportunity for small-time operators. People who care. People who listen. People who have a sincere smile. People who actually answer the phone. People who get back to us right away.

Small is beautiful.

Can you compete? Oh, hell yeah.

I won't make enough

Here is the irony of that statement. People fear they won't make enough money in their own business, but at the same time, complain that their salary is too low.

It could therefore be argued that the exact opposite is true: You won't make enough money staying as an employee.

As a worker, your income is capped. As a business owner, the sky is the limit.

The reason employee salaries are capped is that employers make their profit on the backs of their workers, billing out labor at a much higher rate than what they're paying for it.

As a business owner, you'll be able to charge a lot of money if your customers believe you're worth it. You won't be offering your services at a low hourly rate. You'll be charging based on perceived value to the customers you serve.

Getting work is too hard

This excuse has been around for eternity. It's just too difficult to market a business these days. Getting work is hard.

But consider this. If you apply for a job, you'll be competing with hundreds, if not thousands of people. As a self-employed person or small business owner, on the other hand, competing for a contract, you might be up against five to 10 other firms.

Which is more difficult? Competing with thousands, or just a few?

As someone who owns a service business, you likely won't be obtaining sales from cold calls or advertising. It will start with a well-written proposal, which, if accepted, will lead to a contract with a client who – if you do a great job - will spread the word about you.

That is the formula I am recommending in this book, and in a later chapter, I will explain how you can produce a winning proposal, and then how you should operate your business in its very early stages in order to promote word of mouth

Getting work is only hard if you have no idea what you're doing. And most people don't.

You deserve it

The excuses and false beliefs I have just outlined in this chapter only scratch the surface of why people don't start a business. There are, in fact, millions of excuses.

My hope is that by debunking the misinformation and drawing attention to reality, you will now have more confidence to proceed.

You deserve it.

Let's therefore dispense with the time-wasting excuses and get down to work.

5 YOUR SERVICE BUSINESS

You're sitting at your kitchen table, contemplating what business you'll start.

The logical answer might be to do whatever you did as an employee – but, that's not always a good idea. You may have hated what you were doing, or, if you're being totally honest with yourself, you may not have been that good at it.

It has been said that we need to follow our passion. Again – not always a wise route if what you love to create is something people don't want.

The way I like to word the all-important question of what business to start is to ask yourself:

"What can I do that interests me and that customers will likely benefit from?"

Make it a service business. Service businesses are the easiest to start, requiring little to no money. Product-based businesses and manufacturing are high risk ventures the first-time entrepreneur should avoid.

The kind of service business I am referring to involves no capital expenditure, other than perhaps the purchase of a laptop computer. It's the kind of business that needs only your brain, your energy, and in some cases, your brawn.

A car repair shop and dry-cleaning business are both services, but expensive to launch.

Think of a business that relies primarily on you and can be launched for under $500.

You'll find many lists on the Internet of businesses that would fall under this category. They include such endeavors as "social media management" "writing" "consulting" "coaching" "computer programming/coding" "painter" and even "voice-over work."

We could also add some of the trades, those which may not require a huge investment in tools. Basic services that every company needs, such as cleaning, are certainly on this list.

But there are many opportunities "outside of the box" as well. These would be services you might not immediately think about but have enormous potential.

Here is a key question:

"Is there anything I can do that other people don't like doing, or find hard to do?"

Event planning is a service that exists because it's time consuming - having to call hotels, catering companies and organizing everything. It's something a lot of people could do, but don't particularly want to do.

Take a boring, questionable or troubled industry and make it professional and exciting

There are whole industries out there that are struggling with credibility. These are businesses known for doing a poor job and are populated by questionable operators.

In a recent news report, a moving company decided they didn't want to transport all of their customer's furniture so they just dumped all of it on the side of a street. It's stories like that which give all moving companies a bad name, creating an opportunity for someone to "professionalize" their local moving business.

Things that big companies don't want to do

My very first business is what I called "resume auditing." I had read an article one day that said hotels were finding it tough hiring people they could trust (a problem which remains to this day). I loved doing research (and still do), so I offered my services to check up on what job applicants were claiming in their resumes. To my absolute surprise, I had major hotel firms knocking on my door because it was something they needed, but didn't want to do.

You'd be amazed what ideas you can come up with by reading the headlines. They are filled with industry headaches. Maybe you can help with those headaches.

Make people happy

We hear almost daily about how unhappy society has become. Millions are struggling with depression and hopelessness. A recent study in the UK claimed that over 80 per cent of all millennials believe their lives are meaningless.

We're in desperate need of beautiful things to put a smile on our faces and warm our troubled souls. In my book "10 Amazing Ways to Beat Hopelessness, Anxiety and Fear," I propose that people who are feeling down – or anyone for that matter – exercise their creative juices.

If you love art, crafts and beautiful things – offer your creations to the world. It's debatable whether "arts and crafts" can be categorized as a "service" but if you're making others happier, then you are "of service" to them.

I had suggested to a wedding photographer friend of mine who was struggling with her business, to introduce a new service of "fun" wedding photographs. Wild stuff. Take pictures of the bride and groom jumping up and down on a bed. Be creative. Be fun. People really need more fun in their lives. And they're willing to pay for it.

One artist I saw online used the brilliant tactic of producing all original work and rather than showing pictures of abstract paintings he was selling, he showed those that had already been sold, proving to potential buyers that what he did was considered of value by other people.

Return as a contractor

The most successful transition from employee to owner I had ever made involved the very same company I had quit. While employed there, I was a writer. But when I left, there was a pretty big hole in the editorial department. You guessed it. They hired me back a few months later, but this time, I was a contractor and I charged a lot more than what I made as an employee.

I took this a step further and contacted other previous employers with whom I had an amicable parting. A few of them also hired my services, and before I knew it, I was so busy that I had to hire an assistant writer.

Can you knock on the door of past employers who know and like you?

Just act

As famous entrepreneur Richard Branson would say – "Screw it. Just do it."

I can't tell you what business to start. But I can tell you that whatever idea you choose, it's not so much what you're doing, but *how you're doing it.* You could take any venture at all – any business – and make it better, more attractive, more exciting and more reliable than people are used to.

Don't spend all of your time thinking and planning, and never acting. That's what most people do – they procrastinate and make up excuses as to why they can't get started. Once you have an idea, not only for the business activity itself, but how you can make that business "different" "interesting" and better in some way compared to other similar businesses – then get going.

If you hit roadblocks, don't worry. You will simply change direction and fine tune as needed. What's the worst that can happen? Yes, you may need to quit and start over, or go back to the job market. But at least you gave it a shot, and if you stick to my recommendations in this book, you won't lose a lot of money.

Do you want to lead a life of regret? You do not.

One last "but" - what if I'm not good enough?

I'm sticking this at the end of this chapter because despite everything I have just said, you might still be sitting there in a puddle of self-doubt.

So many people avoid the option of running their own operation because they feel they have nothing to offer the world. Or, they feel they're simply not very good at anything. (Why then should anyone hire you as an employee?)

It's a sad commentary on society that we have produced a generation of people with low self-esteem. Years of beating down on employees has many of us believing that the best we can do is type an email. And even then, it's not a particularly good email.

The truth is – we all have something to offer. We're all entitled to a chance at developing a better life.

When I began my writing business, I wasn't a particularly good writer. But I could listen well.

It may seem overly simplistic to say that I built a business almost entirely on just my listening skills, but that's exactly what happened.

A friend of mine is a consultant with an amazing ability to come up with ideas to solve client problems. He's a generalist – not specializing in any particular field. But he happens to be good at generating ideas.

Today – clients are looking at soft skills as much as hard technical qualifications. In some ways, what they're looking for in employees is also what they look for in the contractors and small businesses they hire.

Clients may be looking for certain credentials as well, so don't be shy about telling prospects about your degrees, certificates and awards.

Other times – your target market is interested in your experience.

Expertise is always high on the list. And what is an expert? Somebody who knows a lot about a particular field of endeavor. Not everything – just a lot. Study and learn as much as you can about your craft and soon enough, you'll be the expert that clients want.

When I speak to clients, I always acknowledge their expertise as well. This is often an area ignored. As a business owner, you may feel that you're the one with all of the answers. In fact, your clients need you to listen to their experiences and knowledge as well, in order that you have all of the information needed to serve appropriately.

There is another reason to acknowledge client expertise: their ego. Clients have feelings too. Remember, when you're speaking to a client, you're usually talking to what you used to be – an employee - someone who likely isn't getting any validation from their boss.

If you give them the respect they may be lacking in their organization, you're more likely to get the contract.

Very often, and this may sound a little crazy, but it's so true – companies will hire your business because they like you.

The "likeability" factor applies when managers hire employees, but it's also applicable to the hiring of businesses, freelancers and contractors.

Never underestimate the power of a smile.

In all cases, the bottom line comes down to this: can you get the job done, and can you do it within budget?

Stop with the self-doubt.

6 THE TRANSITION

The next phase of our journey looks at your transition between being an employee and becoming an owner. This can be an awkward time. It requires planning, in addition to a mind shift, not only on your part, but that of your spouse or partner. There will be changes in how you work, live and manage your primary relationships.

I've outlined the transition phase into these areas of recommended activity.

1. Create a Buffer

Once you've decided that you'll launch your own business, you absolutely need to pack away as much money as you can in order to cover living expenses in that critical first six months to one year when the business is not bringing in any money. Ideally, you'll have a full year of expenses in the bank to give your operation time to gain traction. If you can't do a year, cover as many months of expenses as you can. It's going to make the transition so much easier which will reduce your stress. You're going to need all of your energy to focus on building the business, and not worrying about paying bills.

At my lowest point, I had only $20 left in my bank account. I was just three months into my business and my first few clients owed me money. The anxiety I experienced waiting for that money was incredible, and I'm pretty sure it's why I ultimately developed type 2 diabetes. I don't want you to go through that (diabetes, which can be life threatening, is caused by a variety of factors and high stress is one of them). If you're lucky and you secure a few contracts right away, it's still going to be a while before you complete the work, invoice, and ultimately get paid. It's a process that can typically take four to five months.

It helps if you have a spouse or partner with a good job. If you're alone, then packing away living expenses is not an option. It's a must. Even if you're happy at your job and feeling secure, that day is likely to come when you're let go. Protect yourself. I can't emphasize that enough.

Remember – it's about risk reduction.

2. Become part-time

This may not be possible, but find out if your existing employer will allow you to go part time as you transition to business ownership. This will free up time to start the business, and allow you to keep receiving a paycheck - at least until the money starts coming in from the business, at which point you can resign from the job. This is a strategy I used and it worked quite well, although admittedly, balancing both a job and starting a business can be exhausting.

3. Send out proposals

If you're fortunate to have a company that lets you work part-time for a period (or agrees to give you contract work), make good use of that time and send out proposals to prospective clients (while you are still employed). When I began my writing and research firm, I sent out five proposals within a span of two months. I managed to win two of the five and the dollar value of those first two contracts equaled about 6 months of my part-time salary. The idea here is to line up work before you quit your job.

4. If you're fired or laid off

Of course, if you are terminated from your employment, you won't have the luxury of preparing your business. Getting dismissed is traumatic and most people take a while to recover. I would be a fool to recommend you start sending out proposals the day after you're fired (although that wouldn't hurt). Take what time you need to recover emotionally. You may need to go on government assistance for a period to help transition (which I did at one point). But never lose sight of your goal - to get off assistance and start a business.

5. Get your spouse or partner on side

You're definitely going to need support from your significant other. Be up front with him or her, and explain that the "job" thing isn't working for you. Your partner will be most worried about money so sit down and create a financial plan that both of you can live with. There will need to be some expenses cut and you may need to dig into the family emergency fund. If you work well with your partner, see if she or he is willing to help out with the business. You're in this together. You can also give yourself a time limit, as I did, informing my wife that I was giving myself six months to generate enough money to at least pay half of our bills. Of course, you're likely to be working some long hours, so let your other half know that as well - which brings me to the next point.

6. Don't neglect your family

Most new business owners live and breathe their new business. It can keep you awake at night, pre-occupy your mind to the point where you stop listening to people, and it can take valuable time away from family relationships. In far too many cases, marital break-up is the result. Resist the urge to go all out on a 24/7 basis. I had actually scheduled my family time. You should too. Put it right into your calendar and stick to it. You're asking your other half for support. Be sure it's reciprocal, or their support will diminish.

7. Reach an understanding

Most new businesses are operated from home (and after 30 years, I still do most of my work there). But your spouse may view this as a great opportunity to get you to do a few more chores around the house (which you've been putting off). Make it clear that whatever hours you choose to work are strictly for just that - work. And you'll be happy to take care of house-related items outside of those hours. Your spouse needs to know that your business is not a low priority experiment. It is, in fact, your livelihood and your spouse will have as much to gain as you, when things go well.

8. Managing friends

You'll be working long hours in those first few weeks and months (and for most small business owners, the long days will persist), but your friends may not be understanding. They'll still expect you to join them for a game of golf, a few beers or just to pop over and say hello. On a particularly stressful day, I cruelly told a buddy of mine, "I don't need friends, I need money." And that pretty much sums up the attitude of anyone who is struggling to build a business, truth be told. I can tell you now that you will lose friends. Only those that support you 100 per cent will stick around. Yes, you'll have less time for socializing. But be sure to make at least some time, especially for those you value the most, because while you may now be in business, you still need to have a balanced life.

9. A crash course in everything

What I found most amazing about starting a business was all of the many things I had to learn. My brain hurt from the bombardment of information. Running your own show means wearing all of the hats, especially at the start. Many people don't know this, but Amazon founder Jeff Bezos personally stuffed books into boxes in those very early days of the giant online retailer. You'll be stuffing boxes too, doing paperwork, accepting client enquiries, overseeing projects, sending out invoices - you name it, you're going to be doing it. And you'll need to learn how to do it right. Know that in the early days, your mind will need to be a sponge.

10. Take care of yourself

In the transition phase between employer to owner, you must take care of yourself. It'll be easy to work without sleep, without eating and often, without speaking to anyone. Many a start-up business owner has burned out before she or he even got going. Get the sleep you need. Eat well. Exercise. See your doctor once a year. Talk to your significant other every day to let them know you still love them.

Hug your kids. Smile. Stay human.

Your business won't make it without a healthy you.

Get the Feeling

A quick pause here before we go any further. Starting a business sounds like a very daunting task and that's why most people give up before they even start.

The key, initially, is not to think about "starting a business," but rather, to "research a business." That pill is a lot easier to swallow. You need to begin the journey by learning as much as you can about the venture you hope to pursue. Interestingly, along the journey, you may find that you need to change direction.

The important thing here is to use incremental steps of learning, preparing and building, all of which will lead to opening up shop. You can't plan forever, but you do need to plan.

Part of that planning is to visualize your future. You need to "feel" what it's going to be like to break the chains of employment and enter the promised land. These are the thoughts I had put into my head in the weeks and months that preceded my business opening. I'd like you to start thinking this way too.

- It's going to feel good not to rely on anyone else for my living.
- I am gaining greater self-respect and confidence.
- I am just as good as my previous employers and just as worthy.
- If other people can start a business, so can I, since I am no less capable.
- I feel empowered as I edge closer and closer to my goal of self-employment.
- It feels great to be planning this. I have a purpose now.
- I am so looking forward to getting rid of the abuse I have endured from incompetent managers.
- I can feel a sense of freedom as I gear up for my adventure.

Feel your future. Fill your mind with thoughts about how great it's going to be once you're in the driver's seat. Those thoughts will keep you going because as a human being, you are driven my emotion more than anything else. Logic has little to do with what we ultimately decide. We need to realize this, accept it, and then exploit it to our advantage.

You know how you "felt" when your employer treated you badly. You know how you "feel" in a work environment that stifles creativity and treats you as just a number. Now, it's time to "feel" what it's like to be your own boss, in charge of your own affairs, and directing your own destiny.

Get excited. Get pumped. And, get going.

7 HOW TO GET WORK

The single biggest concern people have about being in business is not making any sales. They worry about having too few clients, or having a lot of clients who don't pay. There is a paralyzing fear of just not bringing in any money – of going broke.

What I'm about to say may bother some people, but after 30 years of being in the trenches, I can tell you that attracting customers is simple. You heard me right. It's not difficult, but I need to add this caveat – if you do the right things.

Most people don't do the right things. They defy common sense. They don't plan ahead. They don't think things through. They use hard-sell techniques which may have worked in the 1940s but don't work today. And, they become desperate. (Never panic or look desperate).

Getting the work to fuel your business comes down to these four essential components.

- You must offer a service people need or want.
- You must demonstrate that you're very good at what you do.
- You must convince buyers that you are worth what you're charging.
- You must make buyers feel good about their decision to use you.

Everything in this chapter, if followed, will allow you to easily accomplish these objectives.

You'll quickly realize too that when it comes to marketing, your best weapon will be how you present yourself and your business.

Word of mouth is generated not only by how good you are, but also, how pleasant you are, how much people like you, how easy it is to do business with you, and – how much you seem to be enjoying what you're doing.

Treat clients as you would like to be treated yourself.

The most common comment I get after doing a project for a client is this: "I didn't need to worry about anything. Your business was so easy to work with." That statement compels people to tell their colleagues about you.

Because if people like you, they want to help you. It's a wonderful thing when your clients are doing most of the marketing for your business. You won't need to place expensive advertising, you won't need to do random cold calls, and you won't be lacking for business.

In fact - if you follow the points in this chapter, your biggest problem is not going to be a lack of work. It's going to be having too much work.

Fasten your seatbelt boss. We're about to enter the world of making money.

General public versus organizations

Depending upon your type of service business, you're going to be working either for individual members of the public, or for large organizations, such as national and international corporations, associations and government departments.

Many small businesses, such as cleaning services or any trade, are well suited to serve both categories – individuals and organizations.

But the group you want to focus on is "organizations" for what we'll call "commercial accounts."

It didn't take me long to discover that the smaller the client, the more difficult they are, the least appreciative, the least respectful, and the more likely they'll be of not paying me on time, or not paying me at all.

Even though I ran a small business for many years, the one client group I refused to work for were other small businesses. They would ask for freebies not covered in the contract, and ask for work to be redone which they had previously approved.

I learned that the larger the client (and of course, there are always exceptions) – the more they would trust me and leave me alone to get the job done.

Large organizations take the view that you're a professional and they expect you to do a great job, and if not, they'll simply never talk to you again. Smaller clients, on the other hand, have less money and are extremely picky about how that money is used. As a result, they may not trust you, and they'll want to micro-manage you.

Organizations are bigger and therefore have more money. They're more interested in getting the best possible quality, rather than trying to save a buck or two. But in return for their generosity in payment, they'll demand excellence, professionalism and reliability.

They'll also expect you to solve any problem that comes along and to deal promptly with any issues.

Working for large organizations will up your game, making you want to be the best in your field. You'll learn a lot working for them. And they won't try to "screw you" by not paying you. All of that is worth gold for any small business.

Write a winning proposal

When I first began my business, I couldn't afford advertising, and I was a terrible salesperson (still am). But the one thing I could do is write. As a result, I spent a lot of time writing detailed proposals for large organizations.

Most corporate and government clientele issue what is called "RFPs" which stands for "Requests for Proposals". These RFPs are posted on the web, inviting suppliers, small and large, to compete for the work by sending in their proposals before a set deadline. You may be able to download the RFP for free, but there is sometimes a small fee.

After the closing date, the proposals are reviewed and graded. The proposal deemed to be the best, meeting or exceeding the requirements, is the "winning bid."

The winner isn't necessarily the one with the lowest price. Large clients are looking for the best value for dollar, so if you're charging more money, but also offering better value, you could still win.

Typically, an RFP will be used to award a large contract which can range anywhere from $25,000 to millions of dollars. Many are for opportunities of around $100,000 to $500,000.

You can see here that if you were to win just one of these contracts, your little business would be set for quite a while – possibly a year or more.

I know of one small business owner who, with a staff of only three people, won a contract worth five million dollars. He went from small time operator to a major business literally overnight, kicking into panic mode, having to hire a great many people very quickly.

In my case, I usually apply for and win contracts in the area of $25,000 to $250,000. Of course, I do not win every proposal I write. Some are lost. But business is a numbers game, so the more proposals you write, the better your chances of success.

Keep in mind that the time and effort needed to write a proposal for a large contract can often be the same as a small contract. I once spent a week writing a proposal for a $5,000 contract and lost, and three days in trying to get a $50,000 gig and won.

I don't do any advertising. My main method of obtaining work is through the RFPs.

In certain cases, an RFP will include an extension clause. That means the client can exercise the option of renewing you for another term, if they really like your work. A $100,000 contract over one year might be renewed for another five years, for a total of $500,000.

RFPs are issued for every conceivable kind of service including cleaning and maintenance, food preparation, and painting. That's why it's not a good idea to look down upon somebody who is in the cleaning business. They might well be a multi-millionaire.

RFPs are issued by states, provinces, municipalities, federal governments, large corporations and associations. In some cases, a supplier from one country can apply for an RFP issued in another, but most of the time, the RFP specifies the need for a local or regional supplier.

Small businesses who win RFPs are active and growing enterprises. How can your business win an RFP?

Every RFP is worded differently, but generally, the managers who review your proposal will be looking for a number of key things.

It may take you weeks or even months to write the proposal. My proposals are typically 30 to 100 pages, heavily researched. If you win, it's all worth it. And even if you lose, you can usually reuse some or most of the content you wrote, for a future proposal.

After writing thousands of proposals, I've come up with this short list of how you can produce a winning application in the RFP process.

Be as detailed as possible without using un-necessary language:

A winning proposal is strong on detail. Every statement you make should be supported with examples. Go deep on explanation to showcase your knowledge. Don't skim over things.

Do not repeat the wording that is used in the RFP:

The RFP will normally include a "Statement of Work" which outlines the tasks you will perform. What do most proposal writers do? They simply repeat the list without any added information. You can repeat the list but, on each point, talk about your way of doing things and your understanding of the work.

Draw attention to mistakes and tasks that may not be appropriate:

Don't be afraid to point out any mistakes you may find in the RFP. Organizations will often use an RFP template from years ago. For example, some RFPs I receive for live streaming still reference "flash" as a technology. But flash is generally no longer used because of its security risks. You will gain credibility by drawing attention to errors, or tasks and practices that may no longer be appropriate.

But be sure to back up your position with credible evidence.

Heavily research the client issuing the RFP and relate your submission to their circumstances:

One thing which really impresses is when you take the time to research the history of the organization that has issued the RFP. Sprinkle your proposal with references related to the client. For example, dig into their Annual General Report (you'll find it on their web site) to see what other projects they're working on. Find out what their vision statement is and their objectives for the coming year. Relate all of those tidbits to the work you'll be doing.

Explain your methodologies:

Almost all RFPs will ask you to explain the "how" part of the work and that's where a lot of proposal writers get stuck. What is meant by "methodology?" Sometimes it can be as simple as, when asked to explain how you will stay in contact, to list home phone numbers of your senior project managers to demonstrate your commitment to communications. I use a 20-point checklist to ensure my team never forgets anything. That's the response to "how" we avoid careless mistakes. While the word "methodology" may sound complex, the response can be, and should be, simple and easy to understand.

Include value-added information, even if it's not asked for:

Finally, you can include items in your proposal that the RFP doesn't ask for, if you feel those items will help the reviewers of your proposal make a decision about you. For example, I like to play up my guarantee. While most RFPs don't specifically ask if I have one, it still reinforces my professionalism. Think about what you can add into the proposal to improve your standing, whether or not it's in the RFP.

Unsolicited proposals

In addition to responding to RFPs, many large organizations are also open to what is called "unsolicited proposals."

This is when no RFP is issued, but you send the client a proposal anyway, based on a meeting you've had with the executives. Or, you may be aware of a certain need the client has which you feel you're uniquely qualified to meet.

The ideal un-solicited proposal will be well researched, describing the client's plight and offering solutions. You can also send in a proposal that doesn't solve an existing problem, but would help the client improve some aspect of their operation.

Sending out quotes

Another document that is commonly used to get work is a "quotation" or "quote" for short, normally requested by a potential client who has seen your web site. These are typically only one page, and unlike a proposal that goes into a lot of detail about your company, a quote is just the price that you would charge.

Quotes are usually for smaller jobs, whereas RFPs and unsolicited proposals are for larger contracts spread over a longer period of time.

When sending out a quote, be sure to itemize your pricing so the client can see exactly where their money is going – the amount for each category. For example:

Senior labor (full day): $1,000
Assistant labor (half day): $300
Equipment rental (full day): $400
TOTAL: $1,700

If a client accepts your quote, you can either issue a formal contract, or just have them sign the quote to indicate approval to proceed.

Most clients like to obtain three different quotes (so they'll be contacting two of your competitors). Since a quote is price-based, clients will usually pick the lowest price, unless you've done a great job of explaining why you're worth more.

Would you like a proposal with those ideas?

One final note on quotes and proposals. When you meet a potential client, always ask them about their hopes and dreams for their company or department. What would they like to see happen?

After they answer the question, ask this follow up: "Should I send you a quote or proposal on those things?" There's a good chance they'll say yes because you'll be helping them move their agenda forward.

The more quotes and proposals you have out there, the better. And just because you've sent a proposal on a specific RFP doesn't mean you can't also send an unsolicited proposal or quote on a different subject matter.

If you help clients get what they want, you'll get what you want – a contract.

What about discounts?

Everybody loves a deal.

You can provide clients with a volume discount if they want to use your services for a longer period of time. Many clients will demand a discount before signing.

Most discounting is from five to 15 per cent. If you're already offering your lowest price, letting the client know that usually doesn't work because they still want to see that word "discount" in your quote.

As a result, you may want to increase your pricing overall and then provide the discount, thereby maintaining what was previously your lowest price (rather than going lower than the lowest).

One thing to be aware of when it comes to discounting.

Most government departments and some corporate clients require what they call "price certification" which means they want you to sign to the effect that you're not charging them more than the lowest price you charge other similar organizations for the same or similar work. For example, if you charge one government department $500 a day to clean their windows, and charge another department $300 to clean the same number of windows – then you are favoring one over the other.

That doesn't mean you can't offer discounts. It just means that your pricing has to be fair so that if one client gets a discount, then all clients need to get that same discount for the same work under the same circumstances.

Don't bother with ads

If you write proposals and quotes – you're eventually going to get contracts. The time and effort to write them are well worth it because of the amount of money involved, and the opportunities you'll have to learn and grow.

But if writing submissions sounds too daunting, you may be tempted to just run ads.

Don't.

Unless you're in the retail business selling food or various products for sale, advertising for service businesses usually does very poorly.

If you have a large budget to build awareness, go for it. Even then, don't expect any immediate sales.

Many new businesses try Google ads. I was one of them. I love Google, but after spending a considerable amount of money for a lot of people clicking the ad (apparently competitors and tire kickers), I didn't get a single sale (that could be verified from the ad) and I had to stop, or go broke.

The people making money in the ad business are those who provide the platform for the ads. Not you.

The very fact that you even have to place an ad is telling potential clients that you don't have word of mouth and that you're probably desperate, or not very good.

For the average new service business – sticking with quotes and proposals is by far, in my view, the way to go.

This book is all about saving you money and maximizing your chances of success. In the real world.

Be the subcontractor

There is one way you can acquire a considerable amount of work without writing proposals and quotes, buying ads, making sales calls, or maintaining an online presence – in fact, without doing any marketing at all.

And that's to become a subcontractor for another firm, one that's doing all of the marketing for you.

For example, my company outsources a lot of our labor to a network of subcontractors who we call upon as needed. They don't need to sell or market to us. We contact them.

If you offer graphic design or copywriting services, contact ad agencies to see if you can develop a relationship with them. If you're a camera operator, reach out to photography and video companies that hire freelancers.

Many large service companies hire smaller subcontractors to handle work overflow. If you do accounting, offer to help a larger accounting firm.

Be the help that larger businesses in your field require. Not as an employee, but as an independent business, because that makes you more attractive. You'll be hired only when needed.

Be the back-up

When I first started my business, every single company I approached rejected me. Of course, I was depressed in the beginning. Until I adopted the attitude that "it was their loss". If they didn't see how wonderful I was, then they were being foolish and missing out.

Or, I concluded that I did a poor job of convincing them of my worth. Maybe they were having a bad day and just not open to listening. Or, maybe they just didn't need what I had to offer, and if so, that's okay because why would I want to do work that wasn't needed? All of this to say, I found a way not to take it personally. It was business, and people weren't rejecting me as a person (unless I was rude or unprofessional in some way), as much as they were rejecting what I could do for them.

The real problem arose when my prospects really did need my service, but rejected me because they already had a contractor in place and were pleased with the service they were getting. What to do? I came up with this response: "That's excellent! I am so glad to hear you're happy. But if ever your contractor can't perform for whatever reason, please consider me as your back-up."

You won't believe what happened. Sure enough, after three or four months, at least half of the companies I approached called me back. Their previous contractor had made a critical error, or there was a serious disagreement – in some cases, the contractor had disappeared, maybe they died.

Over time, things change – so I literally waited it out, knowing that sooner or later, something was going to happen that would disrupt the prior relationship and create an opening for me.

You're always the back up in the beginning.

To cold call, or not to cold call?

There are three options regarding cold calling.

Option 1: Random cold calling – No

Calling anyone and everyone indiscriminately, with no advance research on whether they may need your service - is not to be done. You will come across as desperate, and you'll fall into that horrible category called "telemarketing" which will damage your good name. Talking to people who don't want to listen is also devaluing what you offer.

Option 2: Targeted cold calling – Yes

This makes a little more sense because you'll be calling organizations that would likely need the kind of service you offer. When you "target," you have pre-qualified – done your research to ensure that the person at the other end could actually benefit from what you're offering.

Option 3: No cold calling - instead make people come to you – Yes

This is the best solution in which you aren't cold calling at all, but instead, you're creating an environment in which people hear about you through word of mouth, or they see your web site and other communications, which should include testimonials and case studies - and they conclude they simply must have you on board.

When I first started my live streaming business, I was desperate for clients so I called every kind of business, having no idea if they actually needed my service. I was implementing option one – random cold calling. Every call delivered a "no go". Such a waste of time and effort, not to mention, a clear path to reduced confidence.

I came to realize that my ideal prospect was someone who already understood my business, needed the services I provided, and was simply looking for the best supplier.

In other words – I didn't need to find them. They needed to find me.

The cold calling stopped and I went about trying to create buzz so that clients would hear about me. This is a longer process that requires more planning. But it is so worth it.

Having your own business is not about high stress and working like a dog. It's about being smarter and reducing stress, and by so doing, making more money.

I use the web as my external marketing tool (in addition to responding to RFPs). Read on, because now, we'll talk about the right way, and the wrong way, to position your online content to accomplish the task of having clients come to you.

Marketing your service business

There is a ton of information out there on marketing and you could spend all of your time studying it. So, let me share with you what has worked for me in promoting my service businesses. I can do this very quickly to save you an incredible amount of time, not to mention frustration.

No matter whether it's your own web site, a social media platform, or a printed product - you absolutely must begin your promotional content by describing the problem or plight of your poor customer. They need to see themselves before they'll be open to your solutions. That's because they want you to understand them first.

Basic marketing rule:

It's about them, not about you.

For example, the content you could use to promote a business that cares for seniors might be aimed at the family members and begin like this:

"Your loved one is lonely and afraid. They need companionship and security."

Most marketing copy does the opposite. Rather than starting off talking about the customer's plight, it starts off talking about how great the service is. That's a mistake. You have not understood the customer yet.

There is something else I did for years which seemed to have a positive impact on clients. I posted a "code of ethics" on my web site. Essentially, this promised clients that we would be honest with them, listen to their ideas, and operate with the highest degree of integrity.

These can't just be words. You need to live by them.

Business is all about trust between one person and another. If clients do not trust you, you won't last very long (same goes for a marriage, friendship – any human relationship).

Today, people are extremely skeptical. There are questionable operators out there, including some of the largest companies that have been in the news for trying to deceive their clients.

Building trust is important, and the best way to do that, is to position yourself as a company that actually listens to people.

Often, when a potential client calls me, they will tell me far more information than I need to know. I get to hear about every detail of their project, and might even learn all about their lives. In the old days,

I would be impatient and try to hang up on them. But I learned that people want to be heard.

If you listen to them, they'll trust you.

Then, they'll hire you, and pay you.

Deliver pleasant surprises

Another effective way to build word-of-mouth is to deliver unexpected pleasant surprises (the key word being "pleasant").

When my car repair shop returned my vehicle completely cleaned up, looking all shiny and new, without me even asking and without charging me extra – I was elated.

Years ago, a friend of mine asked me to help him market his new moving company. The idea we developed together was to leave a bouquet of flowers in the new residence of his clients. When the moving job was complete, he would go out and buy the flowers and either display them on a kitchen table in a nice vase, or he would hand them to the client.

That one tiny and inexpensive gesture created a major problem – he quickly had far more business than he could handle. But having too much business is a nice problem to have. You can always create systems and hire more people to handle the workload. As I have said repeatedly throughout this book - you can always adjust!

People are strange creatures. As the great Dale Carnegie (author of "How to Win friends and Influence people") once said: "When dealing with people, remember you are not dealing with creatures of logic, but creatures of emotion."

How can you make your client feel good? How can you delight them and put a smile on their face?

The other fascinating thing about delivering pleasant surprises is that it has the hidden benefit of forgiveness. Clients tend to be more forgiving if you make a mistake or forget something.

Add that extra little touch.

Say what you cannot or will not do

It always amazes me how so many people treat their own reputation with indifference. They fail to realize that everything they say and do affects how other people perceive them.

In starting a business, your reputation is everything.

Part of reputation-building is having credibility. Many first-time business owners are so desperate to get business, they'll promise the moon, sun and stars. They'll claim to be able to do everything.

Rather than under-promising and over-delivering, they do the opposite.

If you were hiring someone to fix your car, and they pulled out a business card which said they also do dog-walking, computer programming, and a bit of brain surgery on the side, what would you think?

It's important to let prospects know what you can't do, and what you won't do – and why – in order to gain their trust and be believable.

It's part of demonstrating your expertise and being honest. Clients may want you to do things that you know will be against their best interest. Therefore, they expect you to warn them about what they'd be getting into. In some cases, they may fight you and say "I'm going to see somebody else who will do what I want."

Chances are, they'll later realize you were right and come back to you.

It's about ethics, sadly lacking in most larger businesses that will take money from clients at any cost.

You have an incredible opportunity to stand out from the crowd. To be the supplier your clients can trust.

Use this technique to build your reputation in record time

In the early days of my business, I needed a quick way to show clients I could be trusted. The technique I developed back then is one which you can, and should, use today.

I would set a specific day or time to deliver a quote, proposal or some aspect of the project, and then I would make sure that I delivered before the deadline I gave them.

If I said I would have it for them on Thursday, they got it on Wednesday.

This is easy to implement, but what do most people do? The opposite. They promise for Thursday and deliver on Friday, defending their tardiness with all kinds of excuses.

Given the choice of working with a business that beats their deadlines, and one that is consistently late – clients will pick the early bird every single time.

Consistency and reliability are everything in business.

For phone calls, I would deliberately tell clients I would call them at an odd time, such as 10:45 a.m., not 11.a.m. Of course, in their mind, they're thinking "no way this guy is going to call then". But I do.

Create situations where you can showcase your accuracy and reliability.

Use client names

It was just the other day that a supplier I was considering to hire communicated with me via email, phone calls and a couple of face-to-face meetings. But through all of that communication, he never once said my name.

I developed a dislike for him. He seemed more than capable of doing the work we needed done. But he did not acknowledge me by name. I'm not sure if it was due to his own insecurities, whether he actually forgot my name, or if he was just being inadvertently rude. The reason doesn't matter. (He wasn't hired).

People need to hear their name. It's part of their need to be validated, recognized and, quite frankly, respected.

When first meeting someone, I always ask if they're comfortable with me using their first name, and I make sure I get the name right. I then use their name liberally throughout the conversation, as in "Jane, how about we look at this" or "Bob, that's a great idea".

Address people by name and they'll love you for it.

Look clients in the eye

When people are nervous or anxious, they often look away. They also look away if they're hiding something.

If you never look your client in the eye, you'll be pegged as unprofessional and untrustworthy. And you'll lose the contract.

A lot of people seem to have a problem with eye contact. Younger people, more comfortable communicating through a screen, may not know how to behave face to face.

And people of all ages, sometimes find it difficult to focus on what they're saying, so they'll look all around the room, in an apparent attempt to find the words they're looking for someplace in the air above them.

Worse yet, and extremely common today, is people looking at their phone when they're supposed to be listening to you.

Rudeness has become the norm. But it's still deadly in a business context.

The story is told that one of the greatest listeners of all time was U.S. President John Kennedy who had the unique ability to make you feel as though you were the most important person in the world when he was in a conversation with you. His secret was eye contact.

You don't want to stare at people indefinitely. Look them in the eye, but occasionally blink your eyes, or look down very briefly to indicate you're thinking hard about what they just said. Vary your look, but ensure that most of the time, you have good eye contact.

It's a matter of respect. And no client is going to want to hire you if you show a lack of it.

Look, act and be professional

A big competitive advantage in business, as obvious as this is – is to be professional. That counts not only for you as the owner, but everyone you hire.

I will never forget the time my company had provided support for a conference being run by a client. I had my contractors there, setting up the lighting and the stage. But one of the people I hired had his pants half way down his legs. His pants, what little of them was visible, were also full of holes.

The client came up to me and scolded me, saying if that person was not removed right away, then he needed to go down to the local clothing store and dress in proper attire. There wasn't time for that to happen, so I went up into my hotel room, grabbed one of my own extra pants and gave them to the offending worker.

Ever since that day, I have had a dress code.

In another case, a member of my team got into a heated argument with another team member, in front of the client. Not professional. Not good.

I have a rule. When the client is present, we don't talk to each other. We acknowledge the client, otherwise, we work silently.

We are professional.

I shouldn't have had to include this section in the book, but I've seen way too many cases of unprofessional behavior, so unfortunately – yes, this needs to be here.

As the owner, you set the example. Look good and act professionally at all times, and demand that everyone working for you do the same.

There is simply too much at stake to do otherwise.

Your guarantee

I'm a big believer in offering a guarantee. You can provide a guarantee to clients in a service business just as much as you can with any product.

For example, I guarantee my labor and all of my equipment.

The guarantee states that if anything should go wrong, and we are at fault, I will provide the client with a discount or credit.

In a world full of scam artists and false claims, having a guarantee is that extra degree of comfort that clients are looking for.

Always stay calm

When something goes wrong, it's easy to lose it.

There was a day when my computer was not working and the client needed information out of that machine quickly. I cursed at the darn thing, wanting to throw it across the room, and I didn't sound happy at all. The client, right beside me, became highly agitated and kept asking me: "What's wrong? What's wrong? Oh my, we just can't have this."

If you panic, your client will panic.

If you stay calm, they'll stay calm.

Under no circumstances can you allow yourself to get out of control. It doesn't matter what the problem is – you need to stay cool. And while this should go without saying, most certainly do not yell at and blame your client.

In a world full of chaos, noise, anger and confusion – you need to be that rare person of calm. Be cool and collected. Your client needs that from you.

A stable demeanor, void of temper and high anxiety - is a powerful marketing tool.

Admit mistakes immediately

Eager to please, as a new business owner, I would sometimes try to cover up my mistakes or not admit to them. I felt that doing so would make me appear weak or worse yet, incompetent.

The exact opposite is true.

It takes strength to own up to mistakes. Admission will instill trust. A lack of admission will erode trust.

If a mistake is made that affects the outcome of your service to the client, your client is going to find out about it eventually. The longer you wait to confess, the worse the situation will become.

The truth is, your client, while not being overjoyed, will likely forgive you – if you just admit to it right away, so there's a better chance of fixing things.

Today - whenever I spot a mistake by our team, I inform the client immediately and then outline all of the steps we're taking to make sure it never happens again. Because that's what your client really wants to hear. How you're going to mitigate for the future.

Depending upon the severity of the problem, I also offer to charge less or provide a credit.

And I am often surprised when the client declines my offer of compensation. They're just pleased that I was up front about everything.

Making mistakes and learning from them is not a bad thing. With each mistake, you'll add a policy to prevent it from happening again.

I often go so far as to thank my client for being so understanding, because when everything is said and done, we've become a better company. And the client has greater confidence in us, knowing we've updated our systems and procedures.

Admitting to mistakes helps establish you as more of a partner with your client. It changes the nature of the relationship from potentially adversarial to one in which both sides are learning and growing together.

Become the go-to source

What if you can't provide a service your client needs? Or, if they're asking you to do work that you're uncomfortable doing?

Rather than just saying "I don't do that" - end of story, I take the time to find out if another company may be able to help.

You can, and should, become the go-to supplier for all of your clients. It will make your business more valuable to them.

Sometimes, I will refer the work to one of my own contractors to help build their business. And yes, I will even refer work to a competitor.

It's all about helping the client.

Whenever I do this, especially when I suggest a competing firm, clients are in a bit of shock. They cannot believe that I would protect their interests over my own.

Agree to add-ons, for a price

There will be times that a client asks for something which you don't normally do, but could do. For example, in my writing business, I chose not to design the web sites where the content would reside. I told clients they'd need to hire separate designers because that skill set was outside of my expertise.

But increasingly, due to the heavy workloads most clients are under, they prefer to have a single contract to handle all aspects of a project - rather than taking the time to draft separate contracts for each supplier and manage each one.

Adding a design component to my writing service was not a huge leap. I hired a number of freelance designers and included both writing and design in our packages. Of course, you need to charge for the add-ons, and clients expect that. You should also add a "management fee" because now, rather than the client managing the other suppliers, you are.

While it's good to specialize, it may also be feasible to bring more expertise and services into the tent. It's a win-win because clients have less on their plate, and you make more money.

See if there are other contractors in related fields with whom you can partner for mutual benefit.

Get back to people right away

Oh my. This seems to be a no-brainer – and yet, it's a basic rule that is broken every single day in the business world. We need to respond to client enquiries in a timely manner.

If you take a casual attitude towards communications, you're going to struggle. Eventually, you'll be out of business.

My rule is to return every email and voicemail on the same day. If I'm unable to provide a proper response, then I'll at least acknowledge the message, and let the client know when I'm able to provide a substantive reply. For example: "Can't talk now but will get back to you today at 4 pm."

Many new businesses, burdened by all of the many tasks and responsibilities, fail to get back to clients in a timely fashion.

Yet, if ever there was a priority, this is it.

The term has been used – "If you snooze, you lose". And it's true today more than ever.

A delayed response to a client is a message that you don't care.

Clients start to panic when you don't respond in a timely manner. People, being the odd creatures that they are, will always assume the worst.

You might be in front of your computer screen calmly conducting research, but if you don't get back to clients, they'll assume you're out of business, you became gravely ill or you've died.

Blame today's rapid communication technologies, but there is now an expectation that if a text message is sent, a reply should be made within a few minutes. That may not be right. But that's the way it is.

I hear all of the time from clients who tell me that my company was chosen for a contract because I was the first to respond. And in a surprising number of cases, I'm the only one who responded.

Speed in communications is not a value-added. It's expected.

The only times you should not get back to a client are at night and on weekends – unless of course, the project you're working on requires activity at these times. Answering people during down times will create the immediate expectation that you'll answer every night and every weekend, thereby making you a slave.

You will get messages from clients in off hours. I have one client who likes to toss out ideas so she'll send me emails all hours of the day and night looking for feedback. Just because she emails me late at night does not mean she's expecting a reply right then. She just has to get her thoughts out before she forgets them.

If it's an emergency, or a requirement of the work, respond to the communication in off-hours. If not, make your reply first thing Monday morning.

But know this. Your clients are generally stressed and nervous people. Responding to them in a timely manner provides a layer of comfort.

8 GETTING HELP

Being a lone wolf and doing everything yourself is eventually going to burn you out.

Not only that, but it will prevent your business from growing. There are only so many hours in the day. And you can charge only so much money if you're the only one doing everything.

In this chapter, I recommend how you should acquire help. I'll also warn you about the pitfalls of having a partner and having full-time employees. You'll need to decide for yourself if and when to bring in help. Often, it's going to depend on your cash flow.

Nothing is worse than staying awake at night, on the day before you're supposed to pay your employees, and there's no money in the bank. I was there once and it made me a nervous wreck and a very unpleasant person to be around.

You cannot say to your employees, "Do you guys mind if I pay you in a few weeks from now?"

I will outline how I solved my issues with getting help and how you can too.

Employees versus independent contractors

There is a big difference between an employee and an independent contractor. Many business owners try to avoid paying the tax and other employee-related expenses, by calling their workers "contractors" when in fact, they're not.

Doing this is against the tax laws in many jurisdictions and it's going to get you in a whole lot of trouble. So, let's get this straight right here and now, before we go any further.

The governing body in the United States is the Internal Revenue Service, and in Canada, it's the Canada Revenue Agency. Other countries have similar government agencies to oversee the status of workers.

Generally speaking, an employee is someone who works only for you. The person's salary is determined by you, not them, and you provide all of the tools they need to get the job done. You're in control of how the person will do the job. Employees usually work for extended hours, are paid per hour, and have an employment contract that entitles them to vacation pay and other benefits. They receive a regular paycheck which has taxes deducted.

An independent contractor, on the other hand, is someone who decides what they'll charge. They have their own equipment, and if they cannot do the work you've hired them to do, they have the right to put someone else in their place, providing that other person is also capable of doing the work.

Contractors are usually paid per job, so if you hire them for one day, then you're paying them for just that day. Contractors shouldn't be working in your office because they need to have their own place of work. When you pay a contractor, you don't take off any tax, so they are 100 per cent responsible for paying their own taxes.

The rules vary from place to place, but know that there are rules about this, and it's your responsibility to find out what they are, and to follow them.

If you plead ignorance with tax officials, they'll show no sympathy.

And by the way, you are an independent contractor yourself. You can hire people of the same status as you, and in that case, they are technically called "subcontractors."

Don't have a partner

A lot of people starting out in business are afraid to be alone, so they get themselves a partner – somebody who co-owns the business with them, and in theory at least, shares the risks and responsibilities.

This rarely works because sooner or later, the two of you will disagree and split the company apart or cause it to shut down.

Of course, there are cases where a partnership works well.

Especially if each partner brings something different to the table, and each has their own area of domain. So, I don't want to discourage you here too much. It also depends on how well the two of you get along.

But I'll tell you about two partners in my past and the disasters that ensued. You can be the judge as to whether you might fall into the same misfortune.

The story of Jerry, the insecure drunk

Jerry was legally not a partner at all, but because it was just him and me doing all of the work, he viewed himself on an equal footing. In practice, he was a partner, but technically I was the sole owner of the company and he worked for me.

Most of the time, Jerry and I got along famously and agreed on approaches, which clients to try and get, and what work we would do. We split the tasks evenly and we both attended all key meetings with clients.

But one day, Jerry took me by surprise, bursting into my office in a highly emotional state – one in which he was both angry and on the verge of tears.

He slammed his fist on my desk and said I was an egomaniac who had the nerve to over-ride his decisions. It was an equal partnership he proclaimed and I wasn't living up to my end of the agreement (even though no agreement existed).

A week later, we had an important meeting with a client, but Jerry never showed. Later that night, I went knocking on his apartment door to see if he was alright. He had been drinking over a 24-hour period and was hung over.

I agreed to pay Jerry $10,000 to get rid of him and today, I have no idea where he is, or if he's even alive.

Bob, the office thief

This next case is even more difficult to believe, and as I write these words, I am still in shock, even though this happened years ago.

My communications company at one point had two offices, each in a different city. I managed the main office while my partner Bob managed the other.

I used to call the other office every day to see how things were going, but on one day, nobody answered the phone. Instead, I got a recording that announced a different company name. I believed that I had mis-dialed so I checked the number, and sure enough it was the correct number.

My partner had decided, without telling me, that he had converted the satellite office of our firm, into the main office of what was now his company.

Bob and I were friends for 20 years to that point. We knew each other from our days working together as employees in the same company. His decision to cut our corporate ties and go it alone, too afraid to let me know, destroyed the friendship. Today, we no longer speak to each other.

Be very careful who you choose to have as a partner. If at all possible, don't have one at all. If you feel that you absolutely need to have a partner, put all of the parameters of the relationship in a legal agreement.

Having more than one chief usually doesn't work.

Beware the employee

It's rare that you'll need to hire employees on day one, or even in the first year of your business. But as you acquire more clients and contracts, and the money starts flowing, you'll need to consider hiring part-time or full-time employees.

Most small businesses end up hiring an administrative assistant, or other key position as an employee, but use contractors paid on a per job basis for the technical work. (More on hiring contractors coming up).

There was a time that my business was so busy, hiring employees was inevitable.

But as a new business owner, I was not prepared to be a manager of people.

In fact, I was likely the worst manager on the planet. I had broken all of the rules. I hired friends. I hired people I felt sorry for. I never checked references. I didn't use a recruitment agency that could do the interviews and screening for me. I foolishly hired some people on the spot.

If you get anything out of this chapter – it's this: A single "bad" hire can destroy your business in no time flat.

Here are the incredible true stories of Fred and Sally. I blame myself for what happened because I was responsible for hiring and training. My hope is that you'll learn from my mistakes and become obsessively careful when taking on anybody to work for you.

Fred the graphic designer

I should have known something wasn't quite right with Fred when during the interview, I revealed the starting salary was only $12 an hour - considered low for the position to which he was applying, that of a graphic designer (money was tight at the time). Fred looked at me and said "fantastic!". I replied "You think $12 is fantastic?" (and thought to myself, is this guy for real?). Fred, who was desperate to be hired, said yes - so I believed I had found that special, rare individual who had skill, but no desire for a lot of money. He's a keeper I thought, so I hired Fred (without checking references).

At the time, the place for my graphic design business was the entire top floor of an old house. The rent was good, and I liked all the different rooms that I converted into offices. The house even had a shower.

One day I got to the office very early at 6 a.m. only to spot Fred walking around the office naked. And wet. He had used the shower and upon seeing me, quickly covered up. When I asked what he was doing in the office at 6 a.m., he showed me a broom (pushed in front of my face). Fred explained that he was cleaning up the place - you know, just starting the day off right.

I quickly concluded that Fred was one of the most insecure people on earth. He reasoned that if he could prove to me that he was more than just a designer - that he was, in fact, also a janitor - then I was getting a lot for my measly $12 an hour, and why would I even entertain the idea of ever getting rid of him?

But the use of the shower, unsightly view of Fred's large buttocks in front of me, and having a broom shoved before my eyes - was just the beginning. Driving by the house one night, I noticed a light was left on in one of the offices. I pulled into the parking lot and went into the office to turn off the light, when I then heard a strange sound. It was Fred snoring. I looked down and saw him crunched in a sleeping bag on the hallway floor.

Fred had moved in.

"My wife kicked me out and I had no other place to go," he explained with a sad and stressed look on his face.

As a new business owner, I wanted to avoid a reputation of cruelty and the truth is, I felt bad for Fred. So, I agreed to let him stay for a few nights until he found a place of his own, which he did.

For a while, all seemed good with Fred. A number of clients liked him - he was personable, friendly and always helpful.

But things took a scary turn for the worse when Fred choked on a piece of broccoli while eating lunch at his desk. To my amazement, another employee named Jane, a small thin woman who rarely spoke, jumped from her desk, ran to Fred and attempted to perform the Heimlich maneuver. Picture a tiny woman grabbing the mid-section of a 200-pound man choking on food, and almost lifting him into the air, then body slamming him back down. (The maneuver involves abdominal thrusts designed to lift the diaphragm and expel whatever happens to be lodged inside the air passage).

Jane was not successful. I could see Fred's face turning red as Jane tossed his limp jelly-like body around like a wild animal would attack its prey. We called an ambulance and got Fred to a hospital where he was treated.

It would be a short time later that a major showdown between myself and Fred, the broccoli choking graphic designer, would unfold.

I had discovered that Fred was stealing from us. At first, and this will sound ridiculous, but Fred had taken a pair of scissors. (Why scissors, I will never know but Fred wasn't your average thief). The stealing would escalate, moving on to paperclips. Then toilet paper (which was not good).

Fred had to go.

After I had fired Fred, I noticed something else had gone missing. It was project work for a major client, all on a USB stick which Fred grabbed prior to leaving the office.

When I contacted Fred and asked for the stick to be returned, he tried to blackmail me, asking for $5,000 in return for the stick. I reluctantly agreed and managed to protect our relationship with the client.

Fred was not a bad guy. But he was troubled. And if I had really done my job as a business owner, I would have arranged for him to get help.

But the story of Fred is a yellow flag to all new business owners about the risks involved in hiring the wrong person.

Sally the speller, sort of

Next, I will introduce you to Sally, the administrator I had hired to help us with our mail-outs. I put Sally in front of a computer and told her to double check all of the names and addresses we had on file.

After a couple of days, Sally proudly announced that she was all done and I could have a look at the list. To my absolute horror, all of the names had been misspelled. And badly. Rather than confirming that we had the correct names, Sally had changed the names.

The name "Jonathan" became "Jonas". The name "Richard" became "Rico". The name "Shirley" became "Surely".

I was in a state of shock. I looked at Sally and asked her why she changed everybody's name to a different spelling. Her response (get ready for it): "I was improving the spelling." (Sally was not dyslexic. She actually believed the names had to be "updated").

I had never heard of anything so ridiculous in my life. You cannot improve upon the spelling of somebody's name. It's their name, for goodness sake.

Sally, as it turns out, was extremely deficient in spelling and this did not bode well for her career as an administrator.

After I let Sally go, she would contact me again, years later, still hoping to get work as an administrative assistant. I declined the offer.

It's not about how many employees you have

Never hire employees so you can brag about having a larger company. A friend of mine who was always competing with me, would often boast that he had more employees than I did – that somehow this meant he was more successful.

In fact, it just showed he was a fool. His income was far less than mine, even though he had more full-time employees. Sure enough, he eventually could no longer afford to keep his employees. Rather than admitting he was wrong to hire so many people and repair the damage by scaling back, he had to declare bankruptcy. He had lost everything.

It's not about how many people you have working for you. It's about how much money the company is making.

The contractor-based model

There is a way you can set up your business so that people are "contracted" only when they are needed. I referred to independent contractors at the start of this chapter and compared their status to that of employees.

Using a contractor system avoids all of the complications of an employee-based model. For example, in letting go of Fred and Sally, there was a legal procedure that had to be followed and a considerable amount of paperwork, not to mention the payout of severance.

But before you hire people on a contract basis, you'll need to check with the tax department of your jurisdiction to ensure their status fits the legal definition of an "independent contractor."

There are two main advantages to using a contractor system. If you make a mistake and hire someone who is not appropriate, it's easy to end the relationship because you simply don't have that person on any more jobs. Contractors are also much easier on your cash flow, because unlike employees who need to be paid even if no money is coming into the company, contractors are only paid when they work, on a per job basis.

There are disadvantages to contractors too. Refer back to the start of this chapter. There are cases when you cannot hire a contractor and the worker must become an employee.

But for most new businesses, using a contractor-based model only, or a combination of employees and contractors (depending upon the nature of each position), will carry a lot less risk.

9 MONEY MATTERS

We now come to the matter of money.

Money and cash flow are things many people do not understand. They act as though money grows on trees, and they're shocked when money seems to disappear.

As an employee, your income was limited. As a business owner, there is no limit to how much money you can make. Your income is determined largely by the demand for what you do, and how good you are at doing it.

Charge a lot

So, the big question is – how much do you charge?

You'll need to know the going rate for your industry and price accordingly. But one thing you definitely don't want to do is position yourself at the low end of the market. You don't want to be the supplier who is constantly lowering their price in a desperate attempt to get and keep clients.

If your competitors try to beat your low price, and you lower your price again – we now have a race to the bottom. Rather than offering a service, you'll be offering a commodity which is something clients buy strictly on price because all of the suppliers are offering basically the same thing.

When you compete on price, you're seen as the "cheap" company. Clients who have money won't hire you because they're looking for the best, not the cheapest. People gauge how good a company is partly on what it charges. Low pricing translates into the "basics" with no added value. High pricing sends the message that you're very good at what you do.

In this context, price can be used as a marketing tool.

Compete on quality, reliability, speed and innovation. If you provide a premium service, you can charge a premium price. Go for the high end of the market – clients who want the very best.

Your price should factor in all of your expenses plus a healthy profit for yourself, known as the "mark-up." How much profit? That's up to you, but remember, you might run into a slow spell so if your mark-up is too little, you may run out of money to cover those slow periods.

My business is seasonal. Nobody contacts us in the summer months, so I need to make sure that I'm making enough money to pay all the bills for those two months, without any new money coming in. (I wrote this book in the summer, the only time I had available).

Depending upon the type of business you're in, your expertise, and how badly clients want you – you can charge anywhere between approximately $200 and $2,000 a day (in North America). That's for you personally when you're on a job. If you have equipment and contractors, you'll be billing out your entire company at much higher amounts.

A friend of mine is a videography and film director who bills out his small company at $15,000 a day. Of that, he's making in the area of $7,500 a day.

Is he worth that kind of money? His clients think so. He produces amazing work.

Your price is a reflection of what your worth to your clients. And it's often about "wowing" clients – giving them more than they expect.

Many new business owners make the mistake of charging too little. They're not confident that anyone will want what they're offering, so they practically give away their services. And some actually do offer their services for free - hoping that someone - anyone really - will hire them, and hopefully see their worth so they can eventually charge something.

It's a horrible strategy to use, because once you're known as a "freebie" company, people will see you more as a "hobbyist" and nobody is going to want to pay you in the future. You'll be among the many businesses that disappear in the first year of operation (more likely, the first month).

Know your worth in the marketplace. Charge accordingly. Increase prices every year to cover rising costs and to compensate you for the experience and knowledge you're picking up along the way.

Do an incredible job. Charge an incredible price.

Have a contract

When a client accepts your quote or proposal, you need to sign a contract with them. (In some jurisdictions, it's the law. You can't do business without a contract).

Sometimes, the client will send you a purchase order that acts like a contract. Other times, they'll send the contract, but mostly, they'll expect you to send one.

The goal of the contract is to make sure both sides are in agreement on all aspects of the job (so there are no surprises) and the contract provides a layer of protection for both sides.

Over the years, my contracts have grown in size. That's because things kept coming up which were not covered. For example, many clients would ask for work not covered in the agreement, and they did this after we both signed the agreement. I therefore included a clause which states "Only work outlined in this contract will be performed. If additional work is requested, an amendment must be made."

You may be surprised that a lot of clients won't even read the contract. As a result, I now have at the top, in big bold red letters: "Please read this contract before signing." (That way they can't come back later and claim to not know about something).

Your contracts should include the following information.

- What work you will perform, when and where.
- How you expect to be paid and how long you'll wait (normally 30 days).
- What actions you will take if you're not paid.
- The conditions under which you or the client can cancel the contract. (I charge $300 if a client cancels on me a day before we're supposed to start working).
- A list of your responsibilities, but also a list of the client's responsibilities.

- A clause that says you won't take any responsibility for work performed by other suppliers.
- Your terms and conditions.
- The terms of your guarantee.
- A clause that makes it clear who owns what (if applicable).
- A clause regarding insurance (so the client doesn't have to worry about damage to their premises or paying for any of your people getting hurt).
- A clause on what will be done if there is a disagreement (for example, appointing a mediator).
- A clause which states what laws are governing the contract (for example, the state or province).

There was a time my contracts had a clause which stated that a client could not sue me under any circumstances. As a new business owner, that's the kind of thing you worry about all of the time.

In most jurisdictions, however, a clause that says you cannot be sued won't hold up in court. Check the laws for your area, and consult a lawyer (this can be a gray area), but chances are, the law will override your contract, and may permit a client to take action if they feel you've done them wrong.

Quick disclaimer here. I am not a lawyer and there is no legal advice in this book. You must consult your lawyer on the issue of contracts.

But I can tell you what I have done. There is a clause that I use which does provide a certain degree of protection and at the same time, keeps my clients happy. It's called a "release clause". Essentially, this states that if I have followed the contract and done everything I was supposed to do, then the client agrees to "release" any legal claims against my company.

The release clause is followed by a "dispute resolution" clause which states if the client believes I have not fulfilled the contract, then the two of us will sit down and work things out.

In my 30 years of being in business, after signing thousands of contracts, there have only been a couple of issues with unhappy clients that I was able to resolve.

In one case, my video company was supposed to record a concert for a major symphony but my camera person couldn't figure out how to use the camera (yup). The contract said we were going to record the concert, but the only thing that got recorded was the camera guy's face stuffed into the camera lens as he attempted to figure out the buttons. In that case, I didn't charge the client anything and they never contacted me again.

Don't be afraid of contracts. Don't worry about what clients "will do to you." Most clients, especially the larger corporations and government departments, are reasonable and believe in the dispute resolution process, if it's needed.

Just be certain you have everything covered in the contract and you'll be okay. Do get a lawyer to approve the wording.

The contract is for your protection as much as for the client. It ensures you will be paid, and that you won't be working like - well, like an employee.

Make it easy for clients to pay you

Make it easy for clients to pay you and never accept cash under the table. Everything you earn needs to be above board and declared at tax time.

Among the options you can give clients is payment by credit card. Many government departments and large corporations now prefer this method. That's because for small jobs, payment by credit card means they don't need to obtain a lot of approvals from upper management. Therefore, by allowing payment by credit card, you'll get work that you might otherwise not.

There are many financial institutions and e-commerce firms out there now that allow you to easily set up an account so you can receive payments by credit card online. The most well-known is PayPal.

The day of traditional paper checks is disappearing. Most clients will want to pay you either by credit card or direct deposit, so they'll ask for your banking information. Give it to them, so you can get paid faster and avoid worrying about checks "lost in the mail."

Also consider asking for a deposit before you start the work. A deposit of 25 per cent is typical. There are two advantages. Firstly, your cash flow will be much better because now, rather than having to wait until a job is finished before receiving any money, you'll have some money right away. In addition, a client is much more likely to pay the balance owed, because they've already given you some money.

What to do if you don't get paid

There will be times you end up with a client or two who just won't pay. In those cases, it's time to get tough.

After they've ignored my phone calls and emails, before I send the case to a collection agency - I send my own message stating that they'll be reported as a "bad debt" to the tax office, affecting their credit rating. I further inform them that a complaint is being filed with the Better Business Bureau and also to all of the industry associations their organization belongs to. My message is copied to the top executives of their firm, including the CEO and Chairperson.

In some cases, I've even threatened to take the case to the media so the whole world can learn that they're a nasty group of people.

Guess what?

Nine times out of ten, I get the money the next day.

Just because you're small and new doesn't mean you have to lie down and play dead. It's okay to scratch such clients off your list and go find better clients.

You and your business deserve it.

More money coming in than going out

The biggest mistake I made when I started my first few businesses was to assume that any day now, clients would come through the door and give me big contracts.

I assumed wrong.

While I was waiting for the money to "pour in" I was spending what little money I had, at one point, taking out a loan so I could pay my people (huge mistake – never, ever do that).

It doesn't get more basic than this: more cash needs to flow in than is flowing out. Not once in a while. But every single week. By the end of the month, your bank statement should show more "credits" than "withdrawals." If it's the other way around, you're in trouble.

Flag this little section with a marker. It's going to save you.

Hire a tax specialist

I will never forget the anger I felt when my then-accountant calmly told me that I owed $100,000 in taxes. I asked why he did not warn me that I was about to get a tax bill that huge, and why he never suggested ways I could try to reduce the amount before getting the bill.

It then dawned on me. He didn't care. The average tax preparer / book-keeper does not believe it is their job to help you. Their only job is to calculate your taxes owed. That's it.

After a few years of almost going broke because I couldn't afford to pay my taxes, I sought help from a tax specialist. When I first met Tim in his office, he looked at me and said "You're crazy." What do you mean, I asked? Tim explained that I had foolishly and mistakenly depended on my accountants to help run my business, when in fact, they had no interest in doing so, and more importantly, most were completely unqualified to do so.

Tim said only a certified tax specialist could really help me. Tax specialists are people who will give you the right advice and let you know if you should or not should incorporate. They'll also set up your books for tax efficiency - all legal.

Never pay more tax than you absolutely have to. Bad tax management will kill your business, and quickly. You can work hard, provide a great service and be doing everything else right. But if you haven't got your tax situation under control, it's all for naught.

I recall many sleepless nights when I fell into depression. What is the point, I asked myself, of working so hard to build a business, if I'm just going to end up going under because of a ridiculous tax bill?

Since my accountants prior to Tim didn't care to inform me that I was likely to owe a lot, I didn't bother to pay monthly payments. Taxes will catch up to you, and it's a shock when you need to pay the full bill in one shot after a year.

If you think the average accountant doesn't care, you'll get an even less sympathetic reaction from the tax department.

Taxes are boring to most entrepreneurs. It's often the last item on the list. But you need to find the best tax specialist you can and hire them to set up your finances correctly. A tax specialist is worth every penny you pay them because they'll be putting a lot more money back into your pocket.

If your accountant is also a tax specialist, fantastic. If they're not, and all you have working for you is a "tax preparer" then fire them and hire somebody who cares about your business and knows how to manage taxes.

Pay your taxes

Speaking of taxes, you do need to pay them. Falling behind in this area, even once, will make it very difficult for you to keep going.

The key to tax reduction is to keep every legitimate receipt for expenses you paid to run your business, more commonly known as "tax write-offs." These include receipts for office rent, credit card purchases and meals with clients to discuss business. If you're not sure what you can claim and what you can't – just keep all receipts and give them to your accountant.

In the first year of my business, I was extremely naive, not realizing that I even had to keep receipts, so when it came to tax time, I had no expenses to claim. That put up a red flag at the tax department which then conducted an audit on my business.

The auditor asked me, "Where are your receipts?"

Response: "What are those exactly?"

"You know, the little pieces of paper you get when you've bought something?"

"Oh, I thought those were garbage. I don't keep those."

I then heard the auditor whispering to his colleague: "This guy is either a master criminal or a complete idiot."

Keep all receipts and all other business-related paperwork, such as invoices, contracts and bank statements. The whole deal.

Good record keeping is a must. It will make your accountant's job easier so they don't have to charge you a fortune for going through a shoe box full of random papers. It's also a best practice when the tax people come calling and ask to see proof of what you've been claiming on your returns.

To incorporate or not?

Your tax specialist will be able to answer this question because it depends on a number of factors but generally, your advisor should recommend that you do incorporate. It's a good idea to keep your business and personal finances separate, and incorporating usually helps reduce your overall taxes since corporate tax is less than personal tax. Incorporating also sends a signal to clients that you're serious about your business, so there is a marketing advantage.

Not all accountants understand, or can work with corporations, so be sure you have one who is capable.

Fire bad clients

Finally, on the topic of money – you may have clients that are costing you money rather than making you money.

They need to go.

Since you're new to business, some people will try and take advantage of that. They might know you have very few clients and consider you to be desperate, likely willing to work insane hours, just to hang on to the contract.

Such people are evil and undeserving of your work.

You might also get clients who attempt to push your price down in return for a favor, such as helping to promote your business to other clients. Don't bite. The chances of that happening are close to nil.

Clients who demand all of your time can destroy your business, because you'll have no energy or time left for your other clients.

A firing is also in order if your client is rude and disrespectful to you or your people. I actually have a clause in my contracts that says I can cancel in the event I find the client to be out of line.

Business is a two-way street. Yes, you need to show respect, but so do they. You're not in business to be mistreated. Been there, done that, when you were an employee.

10 HANG IN THERE

There will be times you're going to feel like giving up. I wanted to give up at least 100 times. Weeks where you don't hear from a single client and the only thing flowing into your inbox are spam messages can get you down.

There will be a ton of problems. I can guarantee you that. But the best way to look at this is to know they are *your* problems. You own them. That means you can learn from them and turn them into opportunities - for learning, and possibly even more business.

So really, there are no problems.

Just challenges.

For a period of time, my business was struggling badly. I decided to play with the numbers. If I could just increase sales by 15 per cent (not out of reach) and reduce expenses by the same 15 per cent (also doable), I would have a net benefit of 30 per cent - more than enough to get me out of a jam.

There is an answer to every stumbling block.

Don't forget. You can always adjust. Tinker. Experiment.

I found that as quickly as things can deteriorate, they can also rise up. One email from the right client at the right moment can change your world in a minute.

Success is often just around the corner. Never underestimate all of your hard work, day after day, week after week, month after month. The results will come all of a sudden.

One piece of brilliant advice I received from a good friend who still works for me to this day, was this:

"Work to please yourself and you'll never be unhappy."

Oh wow. I was so busy trying to please everyone else, I made myself miserable. You could apply this rule to everything in life.

The moment I set up my business to make *me* happy, was the moment things changed. My new, fresh attitude was contagious. Clients want to hire happy people, not depressed people.

My attitude was: "This is what I do and how I do it. If that works for you, great. If not, you'll need to find another supplier."

As a business owner, *you* set the terms.

Resist the urge to customize your service to each client, unless they're willing to pay for that. If I called up Microsoft and asked them to change the buttons on their office programs, how would they respond? They wouldn't.

You have a system, a way of doing things, and if that works for most clients, you'll be fine. The moment you bend over backwards, out of insecurity, to please a single client who is unwilling to pay for the changes, is the moment that client is running your business, and you'll turn into a miserable and pathetic "employee"!

You own the business, not your clients.

Never forget that.

Have fun

We've covered a lot of ground. You'll want to keep this book as a reference as you undertake your adventure in business.

One more thing you can't forget – and that is to make sure you're having fun.

Business is meant to be fun. You should be looking forward to every single day. You should be overjoyed with making a living on your own, being your own boss and helping people – not only those who work for you, but your clients and your community.

As a small business owner, you're driving the economy. While large corporations shrink in size, laying people off by the thousands   you're doing the opposite – growing, learning and contributing to a better, stronger society.

Don't forget to laugh. Love what you're doing.

Life can be really good. When you're an owner.

ABOUT THE AUTHOR

Cory Galbraith is a 30-year veteran of business ownership. He has been fired, laid off, unemployed and was once insulted with a pay increase of just one cent per hour. Angry and frustrated, he vowed to never again apply for another job and instead, created an approach to business that has served him well for over 30 years. Today, he is the owner of an international live streaming company who also keeps busy researching and writing articles and books about business and self-sufficiency.